# WORLD WAR II

**Clive Gifford**

WAYLAND

Published in 2013 by Wayland

Copyright © Wayland 2013

Wayland
338 Euston Road
London NW1 3BH

Wayland Australia
Level 17/207 Kent Street
Sydney NSW 2000

Editor: Julia Adams
Designer: Jason Anscomb (www.rawshock.co.uk)
Picture Researcher: Diana Morris
Consultant: Dr Andrew Dilley
Proof reader and indexer: Sarah Doughty

British Library Cataloguing in Publication Data
Gifford, Clive.
   The who's who of World War II.
   1. World War, 1939-1945--Biography--Juvenile
literature.
   I. Title II. World War II
   940.5'4'00922-dc22
ISBN 978 0 7502 7218 6

Picture acknowledgements:
AP/Topham: 17.
Cody Images: 6, 7, 8, 10, 15, 19.
Mary Evans Picture Library: front cover.
Imperial War Museum, London: 16.
The National Archives, Kew: 24.
Picturepoint/Topham: 4, 5, 9, 12, 13, 18,
   20, 22, 27. 29.
Roger-Viollet/Topham: 21, 25.
Topfoto: 11, 14, 23, 26, 28.

Printed in China

Wayland is a division of Hachette Children's
Books, an Hachette UK company.

www.hachette.co.uk

Disclaimer:
The website addresses (URLs) included in this
book were valid at the time of going to press.
However, because of the nature of the Internet, it
is possible that some addresses may have changed,
or sites may have changed or closed down since
publication. While the author and Publisher
regret any inconvenience this may cause the
readers, no responsibility for any such changes can
be accepted by either the author or the Publisher.

# Contents

# World War II

On 3 September 1939, the British and French governments declared war on Germany. This marked the beginning of World War II, which spread to all continents of the world. It was mostly a conflict between the Axis powers, led by Germany, Japan and Italy, and the Allied powers, led by Britain, the US and the Soviet Union. The US and Soviet Union both entered the war in 1941 and emerged from it as the world's two most powerful nations.

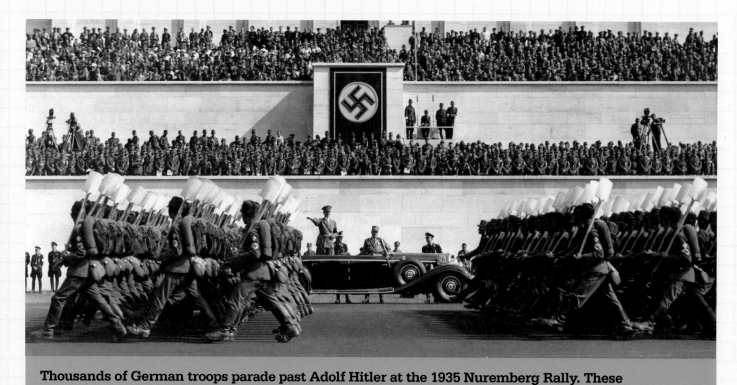

**Thousands of German troops parade past Adolf Hitler at the 1935 Nuremberg Rally. These displays of military might have helped build Hitler's reputation inside Germany before the war.**

Throughout the 1930s, Germany, Italy and Japan had all been making attempts to expand their territory. Japan had invaded Manchuria in 1931 and the rest of China in 1937, Italy had captured Abyssinia (now Ethiopia) and Germany had rearmed its military forces on a large scale. In 1938, Germany annexed Austria and occupied a part of Czechoslovakia called the Sudetenland. At first, the British and French governments tried to accommodate the demands of Germany's leader, Adolf Hitler. But the invasion of Poland by German forces on 1 September 1939 made war inevitable.

By the time that the war ended in 1945, the scale of death and suffering was enormous. Historians believe that between 35 and 60 million people died due to the conflict. Millions more were left homeless, severely injured or orphaned by the war. It was the most destructive conflict in history.

These adults and children were held as prisoners at the Auschwitz concentration camp in Poland until liberation by the Soviets in January 1945. Jews were not the only people to be killed by the Nazis in camps. Roma peoples, Slavs from Russia and Poland, homosexuals and mentally and physically disabled people were also executed in large numbers.

## The Holocaust

A central part of Hitler and the German Nazi Party's policies was the persecution of Jewish peoples. From the time Hitler had come to power in 1933, Jews were increasingly deprived of their rights, harassed, beaten and their property stolen. During the early years of World War II, thousands of Jews were arrested and taken to concentration camps where they worked as slave labourers or were shot and buried in mass graves. The Nazi Party held the Wannsee Conference in January 1942.

Here, they decided on the 'final solution', the extermination of all Jews. Giant camps, mainly based in Poland, were built to carry out the task. These included Auschwitz, Treblinka and Belzec. The camps had gas chambers that were often disguised as showers. Jews were herded into them and killed. Then their bodies were taken away to be burned. The scale of the murder was truly horrific; out of approximately 8.5 million Jews living in German-controlled Europe, around six million were killed.

# Adolf Hitler

After having served in the German infantry during World War I, Adolf Hitler joined an anti-communist political party in 1919. By 1921, he had taken control of the party and renamed it the National Socialist German Workers Party (NSDAP) or Nazi Party. He was imprisoned after a failed attempt to overthrow the Bavarian government in 1923. Hitler wrote most of his famous book, *Mein Kampf* (*My Struggle*) while in prison.

| | |
|---|---|
| **BORN:** 20.04.1889 | |
| **NATIONALITY:** Austrian | |
| **PROFESSION:** Leader of Germany 1934-45 | |
| **DIED:** 30.04.1945 | |

**Hitler attends a Nazi Party rally in Dortmund in 1933. He was a powerful and fierce orator, and his speeches often attacked minority groups for their 'betrayal' of Germany during World War I.**

The Nazi Party managed to seize power in Germany in 1933 using propaganda and speeches combined with bullying and threats. Once in power, Hitler ordered the killing or imprisonment of the people he considered a threat to his power. In 1934, he declared himself absolute ruler of Germany. Hitler's government funded large building projects and gave jobs to millions of workers. But it also suppressed free speech, attacked and persecuted minority groups and built up its military forces. In 1936, Hitler ordered German forces into the Rhineland to re-militarise this part of Germany's. Two years later, Austria was forced to join Germany, Czechoslovakia was occupied and in 1939, Poland was invaded.

When World War II began in 1939, German forces secured victory after victory as they swept through Europe. They also held large parts of North Africa, including Morocco, Tunisia and Algeria. Plans to invade Britain were put aside in late 1940 in favour of heavy bombing of the country and use of German ships and U-boats

Hitler visits troops on the Eastern Front. Throughout the war, Hitler often insisted on taking charge of many military matters personally, as he distrusted many of his generals. Some were too fearful to stand up to him.

(undersea boats or submarines) to cripple Britain's supply lines. Then Hitler turned his attentions eastwards in 1941, invading the Soviet Union, as well as declaring war on the United States. At first, his forces advanced quickly through western Russia. Hitler hoped to crush communism there and gain valuable territory and oil reserves.

The war turned against Germany in 1943 when German troops were defeated in Stalingrad and Kursk. Meanwhile, parts of Italy and North African strongholds fell to the Allies. In June 1944, Allied forces and American troops bombed German industries and cities and via the D-Day landings, invaded northern France. The following month, Hitler just survived an assassination attempt when a bomb was placed in his headquarters by Claus von Stauffenberg. He responded by having thousands of potential rebels executed. By early 1945, enemy forces were advancing towards Berlin from all sides. This meant that Germany's defeat was assured. When Soviet forces reached Berlin on 30 April 1945, Hitler committed suicide.

## The Aryan race

Hitler blamed the defeat of Germany in World War I on Jews, communists and other groups he felt had not given Germany their full support. He believed in the supremacy of the Ayran race (non-Jewish people of northern European descent) over all other peoples and promoted racial purity by various means including the Holocaust and killing of 'inferior peoples' and preventing the mentally ill from having children.

# Winston Churchill

In the 1930s, Winston Churchill was one of the few people in British politics warning about the threat of Germany under Adolf Hitler. The former war journalist, cavalry officer and First Lord of the Admiralty found himself isolated and even ridiculed by some. But when the war began, he was drafted into the British government cabinet, again as First Lord of the Admiralty.

| | |
|---|---|
| **BORN:** 30.11.1874 | |
| **NATIONALITY: English** | |
| **PROFESSION: First Lord of the Admiralty (1939-40) Prime Minister of Britain (1940-45)** | |
| **DIED: 24.01.1965** | |

In May 1940, as Germany's troops swept through much of mainland Europe, the British Prime Minister, Neville Chamberlain, resigned. New leadership was required and Churchill was asked to head a coalition government involving all political parties. He appointed major businessmen and trade union leaders in key jobs concerning industry. Churchill had to make some tough decisions in his first months in power. These included sinking much of the French navy's fleet to stop its firepower being used by Germany against Britain. He also caused a lot of controversy later in the war by sacrificing British forces in Greece and ordering the heavy bombing of German cities and civilians.

Churchill built his relationship with US President, Franklin D. Roosevelt, as he was insistent that British hopes of success depended on gaining strong support from the United States. The pair exchanged over 1,400 messages during the war. Roosevelt arranged shipments of oil, food and economic and military aid to Britain. Churchill had warned of Stalin and Russia's aim to dominate eastern Europe before the war ended,

**Churchill makes his famous V for Victory sign. This symbol became an icon in wartime Britain.**

Churchill inspects bomb damage in south London. Despite advisors urging him to move to safety, Churchill insisted on staying in London throughout the war. He continued to work through bombing raids, often in the underground Cabinet War Rooms.

and Stalin achieved Germany's surrender in May 1945. Churchill's party, the Conservative Party, was defeated at the British general election after the war in 1945. Churchill had been a hugely popular wartime leader but the returning military personnel and many other voters wanted change and voted the Labour Party into power. Churchill returned as Prime Minister in 1951 and stayed a Conservative MP until 1964, a year before his death.

## Making speeches

In his first speech as Prime Minister, Churchill told the British parliament, 'I have nothing to offer but blood, toil, tears and sweat.' It was one of many memorable and stirring speeches he made to the British public during the war including a line in a speech about the Battle of Britain (see panel, page 11), 'Never in the field of human conflict was so much owed by so many to so few.' Despite being sixty-six when he became Prime Minister, Churchill worked exceptionally long hours, wrote his own speeches and believed in the importance of the media to help raise morale.

# Hermann Göring

BORN: 12.01.1893

NATIONALITY: German

PROFESSION: Marshal of the German Luftwaffe

DIED: 15.10.1946

A fighter ace in Manfred von Richthofen's squadron during World War I, Hermann Wilhelm Göring (also spelt Goering) joined the Nazi Party in 1922. He became Hitler's trusted Second-in-Command. Göring held a number of posts in Nazi Germany and was largely responsible for forming the Gestapo secret police. He was put in charge of Hitler's plan to re-arm Germany in the mid-1930s. Göring built up the Luftwaffe into one of the most powerful air forces in Europe.

The Luftwaffe under Göring was a crucial part of Germany's Blitzkrieg, or 'lightning war', tactics. These included low-level bombings and rapid tank and infantry movements that cut through enemy lines. Blitzkrieg proved a major success in the invasion of Poland in 1939 and the following year, when German forces swept through Belgium, the Netherlands and France in 1940.

Göring was confident of his Luftwaffe's military strength and tended to make extravagant claims. He suffered the first of several major setbacks when the Luftwaffe was unable to prevent the evacuation of over 330,000 French and British troops from France to Britain from the beaches of Dunkirk.

Göring was then unable to convert German advantage into victory at the Battle of Britain. Worse was to follow at the Battle of Stalingrad (see page 15) when his claim that the Luftwaffe would supply trapped German forces with 500 tonnes of supplies every day proved impossible.

Following Stalingrad, Hitler relied less on Göring, who was spending a lot of time living the life of a wealthy noble at his estate, Carinhall, north-east of Berlin.

In July 1940, Hitler promoted Göring to the rank of *Reichsmarschall* or Marshal of Germany – a special rank just for Göring. This made him the most senior of all Germany's military men. Yet from 1942 onwards, Göring mostly let people under his command run the Luftwaffe.

# The Battle of Britain

The Battle of Britain was a fight for air superiority over south-east England in the summer of 1940. Göring's Luftwaffe was ordered to crush the British Royal Air Force (RAF), so that Operation Sealion (an invasion of Britain by German forces) could go ahead. Wave after wave of German bombers attacked airfields and other military targets. Despite superior numbers of aircraft, the Luftwaffe were fought off by the RAF and their allies, who had a series of radar stations to provide early warning of Luftwaffe raids. The invasion was called off and the Luftwaffe switched to bombing major British cities at night time. This was known as the Blitz.

A Junkers Ju-97 'Stuka' dive bomber swoops over the River Thames in London. Göring used the Ju-97 in Blitzkrieg attacks. However, these slow and cumbersome planes proved no match for Allied fighter planes such as the Supermarine Spitfire.

There, Göring stockpiled art treasures stolen from the countries Germany occupied. News of his lifestyle angered ordinary Germans who were struggling with the hardships of war.

Göring fled Berlin in April 1945 and sent a telegram to Hitler. In it, he suggested that he (Göring) should take over from Hitler as leader. Hitler was furious and ordered Göring and his family to be killed, but the order was ignored. Within weeks, Hitler had committed suicide and Göring had surrendered to American forces. The following year he was tried for war crimes at the International Military Tribunal in the German city of Nuremberg. He was found guilty and sentenced to death. Göring committed suicide hours before his planned execution.

# Admiral Isoroku Yamamoto

BORN: 04.04.1884

NATIONALITY: Japanese

PROFESSION: Admiral of the Combined Fleet (1940-43)

DIED: 18.04.1943

The United States was reluctant to enter World War II. Japan, however, saw opportunities to capture European colonies in Asia. Japan planned to add these to Korea, which it had occupied thirty years earlier, and parts of China that it had invaded in 1931 and 1937. Japan entered a pact with Italy and Germany in 1940, planning an attack on the US navy at Pearl Harbor in Hawaii. The man behind this plan was Isoroku Yamamoto.

**Admiral Yamamoto as commander of the Japanese Imperial Navy. He was extremely popular amongst the sailors and pilots he commanded.**

Yamamoto had spent all his adult life in the Japanese navy and became a specialist in naval aviation. He had studied at Harvard University and worked in the United States. Yamamoto was reluctant to fight a war against the United States, as he feared there was little chance of defeating such a strong industrial power. However, once it became clear that the Japanese leadership sought war, he began working on a plan in early 1940.

The attack on Pearl Harbor (see panel, right) was a success, but did not completely destroy the US navy base. While Yamamoto's naval forces helped Japan occupy Indonesia and parts of the Philippines, he feared that if the war with the United States lasted much longer than a year, Japan would lose. He planned to engage the remainder of the American fleet in a decisive battle and invade the Midway Islands before conquering Hawaii.

The resulting Battle of Midway in June 1942 did not go as he had planned. It resulted in an American victory and Japan losing aircraft carriers and battleships, as well as more than 220 fighter planes. The balance of power in the Pacific began to tilt and Japanese losses mounted. In April 1943, Yamamoto made inspection tours of his forces in New Guinea and the Solomon Islands. US intelligence captured messages about his movements and planned a mission to kill him, called Operation Vengeance. Yamamoto was on board a long-range bomber when it was shot down by a squadron of American fighter planes. Yamamoto's death was a large blow to Japanese morale and to its naval planning.

The USS Shaw ablaze during the attack on Pearl Harbor. The destroyer was hit by three Japanese bombs during the attack.

## The attack on Pearl Harbor

In late November 1941, a Japanese fleet including six aircraft carriers sailed to a point 440 km (273 miles) north of the Hawaiian Islands. Around 360 aircraft were launched from the carriers on December 7. They attacked the major US naval base, Pearl Harbor, early on a Sunday morning when defences weren't fully manned. The Japanese wreaked havoc on the ships moored in the harbour sinking or severely damaging fifteen US navy vessels, destroying over 180 aircraft and killing more than 2,400 people. The US Pacific Fleet's three aircraft carriers, however, were on manoeuvres away from the naval base, so they were not damaged. Shocked and outraged by the attack, the United States declared war on Japan the next day.

# General Georgy Zhukov

BORN: 01.12.1896

NATIONALITY: Russian

PROFESSION: Deputy Supreme Commander-in-Chief of the Red Army

DIED: 18.06.1974

Born into a poor peasant family, Georgy Zhukov became a soldier in 1915 and fought in the Russian Civil War (1918-20). He rose through the military ranks of the Red Army in the 1920s and 1930s. Zhukov was a keen believer in rapid movement in warfare, using tanks, troop transporters and aircraft. He got the chance to put his tactics into practice in 1938 when he was sent to defend Russia's eastern territory against Japanese attacks.

Germany invaded Russia in 1941, capturing Kiev and threatening the major cities of Leningrad, Stalingrad and Moscow. Zhukov was put in charge of defending Moscow. His forces managed to repel two major German offensives in the winter of 1941-42 and then drive the Germans back with a counter-attack. Stalin appointed him Deputy Supreme Commander-in-Chief of the Red Army. In August 1942, Zhukov was ordered to defend Stalingrad. He devised plans with the Chief of Staff, Aleksandr Vasilevsky, for a huge Soviet attack on the German forces. This attack resulted in the German Sixth Army being beaten and captured in February, 1943.

Zhukov and Vasilevsky worked together again at the Battle of Kursk in June 1943. With over two million soldiers and about 3,000 tanks, this was the largest tank battle in history. The Soviet's brand new T-34 tanks and their general's tactics lead to a German defeat. The war was turning against the Germans as Zhukov commanded Red Army forces, which moved forward through the western Soviet Union and into eastern Europe.

**Zhukov was criticised for his caution early in the war and for later exaggerating his role in some of the Red Army's victories. He was however, a highly successful commander.**

Red Army heavy tanks rumble into the Germany capital city of Berlin as part of the victory column. The Battle for German capital city Berlin was one of the bloodiest of the war – over half a million soldiers and civilians died.

Zhukov's forces advanced through Germany at a rate of 160 km (100 miles) per week and their arrival on the outskirts of Berlin on 30 April 1945 led Adolf Hitler to commit suicide. The fighting in Berlin was intense and bloody, but on May 8 the Germans surrendered and Zhukov stayed on as commander of the Soviet occupation force in Germany. Zhukov gained fame as the general who never lost a battle. Stalin was alert to this. In 1946, the Soviet leader demoted Zhukov to commander of the isolated Odessa region, for fear of Zhukov challenging his leadership.

## The Battle of Stalingrad

Starting in August 1942, the Battle of Stalingrad is considered by some historians as a major turning point in the war. The Germans' advance had been rapid, as Hitler wanted the city of Stalingrad as a base to attack and capture the rich oil fields further south. Intense hand-to-hand fighting occurred through some streets with many deaths on both sides. The onset of a bitter winter, supply shortages and the Germans' use of less well-trained and poorly armed Romanian and Hungarian troops made them vulnerable to the huge counter-attack launched in November by Zhukov and Vasilevsky. The German forces were surrounded by the Red Army and surrendered in February 1943. Around half a million Red Army soldiers were killed stopping the German advance.

# Noor-un-Nisa Inayat Khan

BORN: 02.01.1914

NATIONALITY: Russian

PROFESSION: SOE Operative in Occupied Europe
CODENAMED: Madeleine

DIED: 13.09.1944

During World War II, many more women than ever before worked in traditionally male jobs in factories, transport and in armed forces. The British Special Operations Executive (SOE) worked with resistance groups in Europe who spied, performed sabotage missions and helped Allied personnel escape. The first female SOE agent to work as a radio operator in Europe was Noor-un-Nisa Inayat Khan.

Khan was born in Moscow, Russia, to an Indian father and American mother. Her family were living in Paris when World War II began. She and her brother, Vilayat, escaped France and both joined British forces in November 1940. Vilyat joined the RAF and Khan, the Women's Air Auxillary Air Force. She became a wireless operator. In 1943, Khan began secret training as an agent for SOE's F-Section dealing with France.

Despite some doubts that she was suitable for such dangerous work, there was a desperate need for radio operators to provide a communications link between Britain and the resistance network in Paris. Khan's security training was incomplete when she arrived near Angers, France, in June 1943. She reached Paris and made contact with the resistance network. Khan had barely begun work when a number of leading members of the resistance network were arrested by the Germans.

She spent the summer of 1943 moving from place to place, hiding from the German forces and sending radio transmissions whenever possible.

While working in France, Khan's cover story was that she was a children's nurse called Jeanne-Marie Regnier.

**Armed members of the French resistance take cover behind a city building during the fighting to liberate Paris from German control in August 1944.**

At least twice, offers from England came to fly her home, but she refused, insisting on doing her duty. She did not want to leave the remaining French resistance members in the area without radio communications and she hoped that she could help rebuild the group. Khan was captured in Paris by the German secret police, the Gestapo, in October 1943. She was interrogated for over a month, but is believed to have said nothing. Unfortunately, her radio set and code books were discovered. The following year, she and three other captured female agents were all transported to Dachau concentration camp where they were executed.

## Female agents

The SOE F-section sent thirty-nine female agents to France, of which thirteen, including Khan, did not return. Among the most famous who survived were Odette Samson, Yvonne Cormeau and Virginia Hall. The SOE recruited American Virginia Hall in 1941 to work in France. She avoided capture by the Gestapo for fifteen months. This was all the more remarkable given that she had an artificial wooden leg. She joined the American Office of Strategic Services (OSS) and returned to France in 1944. There, she trained three resistance groups and set up drop zones for British commandoes. The Germans considered her the most dangerous of all Allied agents.

# General Bernard Montgomery

BORN: 17.11.1887

NATIONALITY: English

PROFESSION: Field commander of the British Eighth Army in North Africa (Libya, Tunisia and Egypt) and Italy

DIED: 24.03.1976

After having joined the British Army in 1908, Bernard Montgomery served in India in 1913 and in France in 1946. He also fought in World War I. After the war, he rose through the ranks of the army. At the start of World War II, Montgomery led a division of the British Expeditionary Force (BEF). This force was sent to France, but later had to retreat to Dunkirk. Montgomery gained praise for his part in the organisation of the evacuation from Dunkirk.

In 1942, Montgomery became Field Marshal of the British Eighth Army in North Africa (Libya, Tunisia and Egypt). The region was in danger of being overrun by Germans under the command of Erwin Rommel. Montgomery boosted troop morale and received huge reinforcements. In October 1942, he fought a crucial battle at El Alamein in northern Egypt (see panel, right). El Alamein was the first major land-battle defeat for the Germans and 'Monty', who was decorated with honours, became a hero to the British public. Montgomery continued to command the Eighth Army as they drove German forces back. In November 1942, further Allied forces landed in Algeria to the west of the Germans and, with Montgomery to the east, surrounded the Germans, forcing their surrender in May 1943.

Montgomery took part in the invasion of Italy in the summer of 1943. He was recalled in January 1944 and put in charge of all Allied ground forces that then took part in the D-Day landings

Montgomery, wearing his trademark black beret. He often annoyed his superior officers, but he was highly respected by his men due to his careful planning of campaigns and clear orders.

when the Allies invaded the French region of Normandy. He insisted on increasing the number of the invading forces and clashed frequently with US and British military leaders. However, he was extremely popular with his troops, partly because of the care he invested in their training, equipment and wellbeing. He was sometimes criticised as being cautious before and during battle and suffered several setbacks as the Allied armies advanced through France and Belgium. But on 4 May 1945, he was present at Lüneburg Heath in Germany to witness the surrender of Germany's northern European armies. Promoted to Field Marshal in 1944, Montgomery was made Deputy Supreme Allied Commander in Europe after the war.

**British infantry sprint to the front during the Battle of El Alamein. The victory at El Alamein prevented the German forces capturing Egypt and preserved the important transport route of the Suez Canal.**

## El Alamein

The 12-day Battle of El Alamein was a victory for the British Eighth Army led by Montgomery. The huge reinforcements his army received in the weeks before the campaign would prove decisive. During the Battle of El Alamein, half of Rommel's 80,000-strong army was killed, wounded or taken prisoner. His forces also lost over 450 tanks and hundreds of artillery guns. In contrast, the British and Commonwealth forces suffered 13,500 soldiers injured or killed out of their total number of around 230,000. To Winston Churchill and many others, El Alamein marked an important turning point in World War II. Churchill remarked later that, 'Before Alamein we never had a victory. After Alamein we never had a defeat.'

# Raoul Wallenberg

BORN: 04.08.1912

NATIONALITY: Swedish

PROFESSION: Businessman and diplomat; helped save many Jews in Hungary from execution

DIED: 17.07.1947

Born into a wealthy Swedish family, Raoul Wallenberg studied architecture in the United States in the 1930s before working in Stockholm, Sweden for a business based in Hungary. In the early years of the war, Hungary's Jews were largely left alone, but from spring 1944, when German troops occupied the country, many were deported to camps to be killed.

Sweden remained neutral during World War II, but was shocked by the treatment of the Jews. Wallenberg was sent into occupied Hungary as a Swedish diplomat in July 1944. Together with fellow diplomats, his role was to issue a number of protective passports to Jews, claiming they were connected with Sweden and could not be deported and executed.

Despite major risks, Wallenberg set about issuing thousands of documents and showed great enterprise. With funds, mainly from the American Board of Refugees, he rented over thirty buildings in Budapest. He decorated them with Swedish flags and signs calling them such names as The Swedish Library or Swedish Research Institute. Wallenberg declared these buildings to be Swedish diplomatic territory to prevent German raids. These buildings offered safe shelter to between 10,000 and 15,000 Jews.

Threats to Wallenberg's life were increasing from both the Germans and the Black Arrow Party – the Hungarian fascists who governed Hungary from October 1944. One of the key Nazi leaders involved in the transport of Jews to the death camps was Adolf Eichmann.

Wallenberg gave little thought to his own safety in his quest to save as many Jews as possible from extermination. He was made an honorary US citizen. The only other person decorated in this way was Winston Churchill.

He came to Hungary and Wallenberg met him on several occasions. During one encounter, Eichmann said 'Don't think you're immune just because you're a diplomat and a neutral.' Wallenberg's car was attacked and he was nearly killed just days later. He started moving from house to house to avoid capture or attack.

Days before the Soviet forces liberated Hungary in January 1945, Wallenberg helped stop soldiers killing many of the Jews who still lived in Budapest. Once the Soviets arrived, he reported to them and told his story. It is not certain whether they thought he was a spy, but according to reports he was arrested and died two years later in a Soviet prison. The 100,000 Jews who were still in Budapest when the Soviets arrived had mostly been saved by the efforts of Wallenberg and his colleagues.

**Jewish families being marched out of the Hungarian city of Budapest. Wallenberg often raced alongside columns of Jews being deported, confronting soldiers, issuing documents and securing freedom for as many Jews as he could.**

## Oskar Schindler

Many others risked their lives to save Jews in other countries in Europe. One of the most famous is Oskar Schindler, a German who ran factories in Krakow, Poland. He employed Jewish workers and helped save many from being deported to nearby death camps. He built places to live for his workers inside the factory gates. In 1944 he succeeded in moving his factory and 1,200 Polish Jews out of Poland and into Czechoslovakia. His story was told in a 1982 book, *Schindler's Ark* by Thomas Keneally and, eleven years later, in the award-winning Steven Spielberg film, *Schindler's List*.

# Jacqueline Cochran

Before learning to fly in the early 1930s, Jacqueline Cochran had worked as a child labourer in a cotton mill, a nurse and a beautician. She proved a natural as a pilot and learned to fly in just three weeks. When war broke, she became part of the Wings for Britain scheme, moving aircraft to Britain. In 1941, she became the first woman to pilot a bomber aircraft across the Atlantic.

**BORN: 11.05.1906**

**NATIONALITY: American**

**PROFESSION: Women's Aviation Pioneer Head of the Women Airforce Service Pilots (WASP) (1943-4)**

**DIED: 09.08.1980**

While in Britain, Cochran worked for the Air Transport Auxillary (ATA), which used women pilots to move planes around. This allowed male pilots to carry out more pressing duties. Cochran was determined to set up something similar to the Air Transport Auxillary in the United States. Initially, the male-dominated American military appeared uninterested. Cochran took a group of twenty-five American women pilots back to Britain to join the ATA while continuing to lobby American government and military leaders. In 1942, General Henry Arnold asked Cochran to organise the Women's Flying Training Detachment to train civilian women pilots. The following year, she was asked to form and lead the Women Airforce Service Pilots (WASP). The WASP grew to around 1,070 women pilots and their role expanded from just moving aircraft from place to place. Some worked as test pilots or flew planes that towed targets, to give anti-aircraft gunners practice.

Jacqueline Cochran poses on top of a Lockheed Super Starfighter in which she set new world speed records after World War II. Cochran was also the first pilot to fly above 6,060 m (19,882 feet) using an oxygen mask and broke more aviation records than any other pilot.

Others were involved in repairing planes or training male pilots and navigators. Much to Cochran's dismay, the WASP was disbanded in December 1944. But by that time they had performed vast amounts of valuable work. This included delivering some 12,650 aircraft and flying more than 95 million kilometres (53 million miles). Cochran was awarded the US Distinguished Service Medal and the Flying Cross. She was the first female civilian to receive the honour.

In 1945, Cochran was employed by an American magazine as a reporter. She became the first non-Japanese woman to enter Japan at the war's close, and witnessed the Nuremberg Trials in Germany. Eight years later, she became the first woman to travel faster than the speed of sound when she flew a Canadair F-86 Sabre jet. As a line from her 1953 autobiography explains, 'I might have been born in a hovel, but I am determined to travel with the wind and the stars.'

**Female pilots in the British Air Transport Auxillary were first admitted in 1940. They helped to transport around 300,000 aircraft during the war.**

## Women war pilots

Attitudes to women serving in the war varied between countries during World War II. While women pilots were kept away from combat in the United States, Germany and Britain, Russian women flew thousands of combat missions to repel Germany's invasion. The Russian 588th night bomber squadron, for example, was an all-women group first organised in 1941 by Marina Raskova. Her pilots flew over 23,000 attacks. These were mostly night bombing raids in old wooden Polikarpov PO-2 biplanes. The Germans came to fear the attacks from the all-female squadron calling them, *Nachthexen,* meaning 'night witches'.

# Juan Pujol Garcia

**BORN:** 14.02.1912

**NATIONALITY:** Spanish

**PROFESSION:** Wartime Double Agent for the British
**CODENAMED:** Garbo

**DIED:** 10.10.1988

Born in the Spanish city of Barcelona, Juan Pujol Garcia developed a deep loathing for the extremist politics of fascism during the Spanish Civil War (1936-9), which tore his home country apart. He volunteered his services as a spy to the British in 1940 and was surprised that he was rejected. Showing great ingenuity, he managed to join the Abwehr – the German intelligence service – instead.

Although Garcia operated from Lisbon in Portugal, he was able to convince the Germans that he was working undercover in Britain. He sent back fictitious reports of ship movements and other confidential information by guesswork and watching cinema newsreels. The Germans, in return, gave him equipment and paid him well to enlarge his spy ring by recruiting other spies. Garcia pretended to set up a network of agents for the Germans. At one time, he claimed the network included 27 agents. All of them, from a KLM airlines steward, to a South American student living in Glasgow, were fictitious.

Garcia made contact with British intelligence again in January 1942. This time he was recruited to work as a double agent – in the pay of Germany but, in reality, working for the British. He travelled to Britain in April 1942 and was given the codename Garbo. Over the next two years, he supplied Germany with what they thought was top secret information, and which they often acted on. Some of Garbo's information was indeed true, in order to keep his credibility with the Germans. But many crucial pieces of information were designed by British intelligence

One of the few surviving photos of Juan Garcia, codenamed Garbo. This self-taught spy provided the Allies with a valuable way to deceive German intelligence.

## Operation Fortitude

Garcia's work was part of a large campaign that was designed to mislead the Germans about the timing and location of the Allied invasion of mainland Europe. Operation Fortitude aimed to convince Germany of two planned invasions. One of these was from Scotland into Norway and the other was an invasion of the Pas de Calais region of France by a pretend army division, the First US Army Group (FUSAG). Radio communications and secret documents about the invasions were allowed to fall into German hands. Meanwhile, fake aircraft squadrons, invasion boats and tanks, all made of wood, canvas or inflatable rubber, were assembled on parts of England's south coast. The deceptions were largely successful. Germany stationed many of its forces away from Normandy, the location of the actual D-Day landings in June 1944.

to mislead the enemy. None was more important than helping to mislead Hitler about the Allied invasion of Europe. Garbo was so trusted that he was awarded the Iron Cross medal by Germany. Hitler even delayed sending huge reinforcements to Normandy, because he believed Garbo's advice that the invasion there was just a small diversion. Pujol was awarded an MBE by the British.

When the war was over, he moved to the South American country of Venezuela where he lived quietly until his death in 1988.

**An inflatable tank made of rubber is positioned by army personnel as part of the of D-Day deceptions. Radio loudspeakers also broadcast aircraft noise to trick the Germans.**

# J. Robert Oppenheimer

In the 1920s and 1930s, some of the most exciting new science being conducted was on the nature of atomic particles. Experiments focused on the potential for enormous power to be released when they were split. The United States, with assistance from Britain and Canada, became the first country to build, test and drop an atomic bomb. The scientific head of the atomic bomb development team, known as the Manhattan Project, was J. Robert Oppenheimer.

**BORN:** 22.04.1904

**NATIONALITY:** American

**PROFESSION:** Scientific Director of the Los Alamos National Laboratory. Leader of the team who developed the first atomic bomb.

**DIED:** 18.02.1967

Oppenheimer became a familiar figure to the American public after the war. He lobbied for more funding for science and strict international control on weapons, including the atomic bomb.

The physicist J. Robert Oppenheimer studied in the United States and Germany. In 1927, he received his doctorate from Göttingen University in Germany, the place where he had met famous physicists, such as Niels Bohr. He became a professor of physics at the University of California, where he taught and researched throughout the 1930s. Fears that Germany might be developing an atomic weapon drove the United States to increase its research in the same area.

Oppenheimer was selected to lead the Manhattan Project in 1942 and was appointed to run a new laboratory. He chose Los Alamos, near Santa Fe in the US state of New Mexico, where he had spent time as a child at boarding school. Los Alamos became the most secret installation in the United States, ringed by fences, patrolled continuously by troops and with no one allowed to enter or leave without a pass. Inside Los Alamos, a large team of famous scientists worked feverishly, often twelve or more hours a day, to overcome the enormous

The first atomic bomb was detonated about 600 m (1,969 feet)above the city of Hiroshima. It generated this giant mushroom cloud, which rose more than 6,000 m (19,685 feet) into the atmosphere.

## The Hiroshima bomb

In May 1945, Oppenheimer was head of the Target Committee, which drew up a shortlist of potential sites in Japan for an atomic bomb strike. Various places, largely untouched by other US bombing, were chosen, in case Japan did not agree to surrender beforehand. Hiroshima became the first target. The bomb, nicknamed Little Boy, was dropped from *Enola Gay*, a Boeing B-29 Superfortress bomber. The blast killed around 70,000 people and destroyed almost everything in a 13-square-kilometre area. The death toll at Hiroshima tripled by 1950 because of the vast numbers of Japanese, mostly civilians, who died from injuries from the blast, or of radiation sickness.

hurdles that they faced in producing an atomic weapon. Other groups worked elsewhere in the United States on the project as well.

By July 1945, the first atomic weapon was ready for testing at the Trinity Test site in New Mexico. It was successful and devastating – destroying everything close by, shattering windows 200 km (124 miles) away and creating a giant mushroom cloud that rose over 12,000 m (39,370 feet) into the air. At the end of July, the Allied leaders at the Potsdam Conference issued Japan with an ultimatum to surrender or be threatened with, 'complete and utter destruction'. The atomic bomb was not specifically mentioned. When Japan failed to reply, President Harry S. Truman gave the order and two atomic bombs were dropped – one on Hiroshima on 6 August 1945 and the next on Nagasaki three days later. Japan surrendered less than a week later.

# Propaganda

The communication of ideas and information to persuade people to adopt certain actions or attitudes is called propaganda. It may often involve lies or not telling all of the truth. It is usually performed to persuade people to adopt certain attitudes or actions. During World War II, propaganda was used by all sides, far more than in any previous conflict.

Propaganda was of great importance in the rise of the Nazi Party in Germany. It was used to attack rival politicians and to blame Jews and communists as the real reason for Germany's defeat in World War I. Once in power, Adolf Hitler established the Ministry of Public Enlightenment and Propaganda in 1933 with Joseph Goebbels in command. It controlled the media in Germany, as well as producing thousands of propaganda messages on posters, in film and many other media.

During World War II, the governments of all countries used propaganda on their own people. Posters, cartoons, leaflets, radio broadcasts, messages at the cinema and information in newspapers were designed carefully to prepare the public for war, to boost morale and to encourage the public to do more to help the war effort. Some propaganda messages tried to demonise the enemy – to make them appear as evil and not worthy of any sympathy. Other messages were designed to urge people to take action, for instance urging women to enter work in factories, or families to turn their gardens into vegetable plots. A number of propaganda messages were warnings about conduct and actions, such as the British message, 'Careless Talk Costs Lives'.

Much propaganda during World War II was aimed at the civilians of enemy countries.

It was delivered by radio broadcasts, by air with bomber aircraft dropping thousands of leaflets or smuggled into a country and distributed secretly.

A Japanese propaganda poster showing a Japanese samurai towering over US ships to commemorate the attack on Pearl Harbor. Yamamoto received praise for his planning of the surprise attack.

Some of this material sought to separate the ordinary people from their government, urging them to rise up against their leaders or surrender as there was no chance of victory.

## William Joyce

Regular night-time propaganda radio messages were broadcast to the people of Britain from Germany. Chief amongst the speakers was William Joyce, a member of the British Fascist Party. Joyce's broadcasts attacked Jewish people, poked fun at Winston Churchill and told untrue stories about Britain and the state of the war to upset and unnerve the British people. As many as six million listened in to his broadcasts which always began with the words, 'Germany calling.' After the war, Joyce was captured and tried for treason by the British. He was executed in 1946.

Charles de Gaulle was the leader of the Free French forces fighting German occupation. He made many powerful live speeches and radio broadcasts urging French people to revolt.

# Read It, See It, Hear It

Here are some website links that will help you explore the role of propaganda in World War II further:

http://www.spartacus.schoolnet.co.uk/2WWjoyceW.htm
Read more about the life of William Joyce and his role in spreading German propaganda.

http://www.bbc.co.uk/history/worldwars/wwtwo/churchill_audio.shtml
Listen to radio broadcasts of speeches made by Winston Churchill.

http://www.earthstation1.com/warpostr.html
View this large collection of propaganda posters from World War II.

# Timeline: World War II

| People | Events |
|---|---|

**People**

**Events**

**May 1940**
Winston Churchill appointed Prime Minister of Britain leading a coalition wartime government.

**September 1939**
Germany invades Poland. Britain, France, Australia and New Zealand all declare war on Germany.

**June-September 1940**
Battle of Britain for control of airspace over the UK is fought between German and Allied forces.

**June 1941**
Hitler orders the start of Operation Barbarossa – the invasion of the Soviet Union by German forces.

**September 1941**
First experimental use of gas chambers at Auschwitz concentration camp.

**December 1941**
Japanese surprise attack on Pearl Harbor triggers US declaring war on Japan, Germany and their allies.

**August 1942**
Winston Churchill meets with Soviet leader, Josef Stalin in Moscow.

**September 1942**
Battle of Stalingrad begins.

**October 1942**
Bernard Montgomery's forces secure victory in the Battle of El Alamein.

**April 1943**
Admiral Yamamoto, Japanese mastermind of the raid of Pearl Harbor is killed in US attack.

**June 1943**
The Battle of Midway results in a major American naval victory over the Japanese.

**January 1944**
Soviet troops push German forces back and advance into Poland.

**July 1944**
Hitler survives an assassination attempt at his headquarters.

**June 1944**
D-Day landings involve a huge Allied invasion of Normandy, northern France.

**August 1944**
Paris liberated from German occupation by Allied troops.

**April 1945**
As Soviet troops overrun Berlin, Hitler commits suicide.

**May 1945**
Germany surrenders to Allied forces.

**August 1945**
Atomic bomb designed by large team led by J. Robert Oppenheimer dropped on Japanese city of Hiroshima. Japan surrenders shortly after a second bomb is dropped on Nagasaki.

# Glossary

**Abwehr** spying and intelligence service for the German Armed Forces.

**Allies** those countries such as Britain, Australia, the United States and Russia fighting against the Axis powers.

**Axis** the group of countries led by Germany which fought the allied powers during World War II.

**Blitz** name given to the heavy and frequent bombing raids carried out over Britain by the German airforce during 1940 and 1941.

**Blitzkrieg** German for 'lightning war' It refers specifically to a German military strategy in which bombardment by air is followed by rapid and overwhelming ground attacks.

**civilian** a person not belonging to the armed forces.

**D-Day** the popular term for 6 June 1944, the day when Allied forces landed on the Normandy coast of France and began their efforts to liberate mainland Europe from Nazi occupation.

**evacuation** the withdrawal or removal of troops or civilians from an area.

**fascism** a non-democratic form of government based on fervent nationalism and strong central control under an all-powerful leader.

**Gestapo** the German state secret police formed in the 1930s.

**Holocaust** the mass murder of approximately six million Jews during World War II.

**morale** the mood or confidence of a person, a military force or country's people.

**offensive** a major attack by one side's forces against another's.

**Potsdam Conference** a major meeting of the leaders of the Allied powers to discuss plans about how Europe would be run after World War II.

**radar** an electronic system used in World War II by the British for early warning of aircraft attacks.

# Further information

### Books To Read
*Documenting World War II* [series], various authors, Wayland, 2007.

*Posters and Propaganda In Wartime*, Daniel James and Ruth Thomson, Franklin Watts, 2007.

*History Makers: Winston Churchill*, Sarah Ridley, Franklin Watts, 2009.

*World War II Source Book* [series], various authors, Wayland, 2011.

### Places To Visit
The Cabinet War Rooms and Churchill Museum
King Charles Street, London SW1A 2AQ
**Website:** http://cwr.iwm.org.uk

The Bergen-Belsen Memorial Gedenkstätte Bergen-Belsen, Anne-Frank-Platz, 29303 Lohheide, Germany.
**Website:** http://www.bergenbelsen.de/en

National War and Resistance Museum Liberty Park, Museumpark 1, 5825 AM Overloon, the Netherlands
**Website:** http://www.oorlogsmuseum-overloon.nl/en

### Websites
**http://www.socialstudiesforkids.com/subjects/worldwariifamouspeople.htm**
Profiles of more than a dozen famous people from World War II.

**http://www.secondworldwar.co.uk**
A website with a long biography of Adolf Hitler and short profiles of other important German, British, American, Soviet, Japanese and Italian figures.

**http://www.42explore2.com/ww2bios.htm**
A large collection of links to biographies of dozens of different people from World War II.

**http://www.pbs.org/wgbh/amex/flygirls/index.html**
A fascinating website about women pilots and aircrew during World War II.

**http://www.culture24.org.uk/places%20to%20go/london/tra14553**
Learn more about the Special Operations Executive (SOE) in Baker Street, London, at this website.

**http://www.lib.washington.edu/subject/History/tm/war.html**
A strong collection of links to websites dealing with all aspects of World War II.

# Index